Perfect Cursive Writing

eaf is the canker of heart.

reaf is the canker of heart.

A good tongue is a good weapon.

A good tongue is a good weapon.

One flower makes no garland.

One flower makes no garland.

Prabhas Rao

Hand and Body Position

If you write with right hand.

Paper is placed on an angle to the left . Lefthand steadies the paper and moves it up as you near the bottom of the page. Right hand is free to write.

If you write with left hand.

Paper is placed on an angle to the right . Right hand steadies the paper and moves it up as you near the bottom of the page. Left hand is free to write.

Hold the pencil loosely about 1/2 to 1" above the sharpened point. Hold it between your thumb and index (pointer) finger. Let it rest on your middle finger. Do not grip the pencil tightly or your hand will become very tired. Do not let your hand slip down to the sharp point or you will have difficulty in writing properly.

Swimming is a good exercise.

Swimming is a good exercise.

Cholera is a dreadful disease.

Cholera is a dreadful disease.

Man is social animal

Man is social animal

Lion is the king of beasts.

Lion is the king of beasts.

The moon comes every night.

The moon comes every night.

The stars shines at night.

The stars shines at night.

Udaipur is the city of lakes.

Udaipur is the city of lakes.

Mysore is the city of gardens.

Mysore is the city of gardens.

Surat is famous for silk.

Surat is famous for silk.

Nagpur is famous for oranges.

Nagpur is famous for oranges.

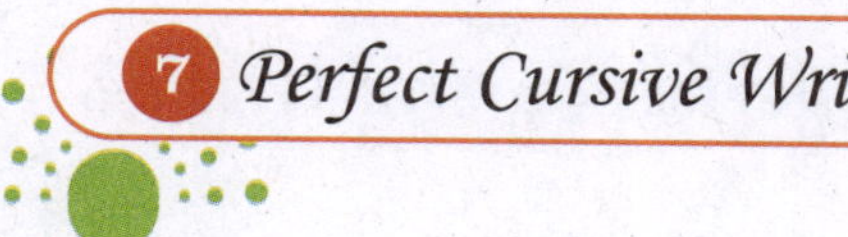

Gwalior is famous for forts.

Gwalior is famous for forts.

Aligarh is famous for locks.

Aligarh is famous for locks.

The Ganga is a big river.

The Ganga is a big river.

Mt. Everest is the biggest mountain.

Mt. Everest is the biggest mountain.

Hard work is our saviour.

Hard work is our saviour.

A good word cost nothing.

A good word cost nothing.

Ego is the root of hell.

Ego is the root of hell.

Truth is the child of courage.

Truth is the child of courage.

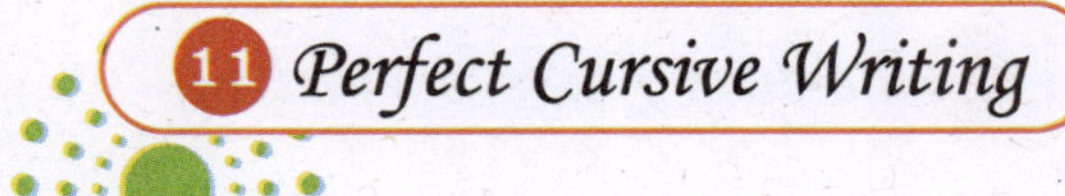

Tommorrow never comes.

Tommorrow never comes.

Habit is the second nature.

Habit is the second nature.

Good health is above wealth.

Good health is above wealth.

Kindness never goes unrewarded.

Kindness never goes unrewarded.

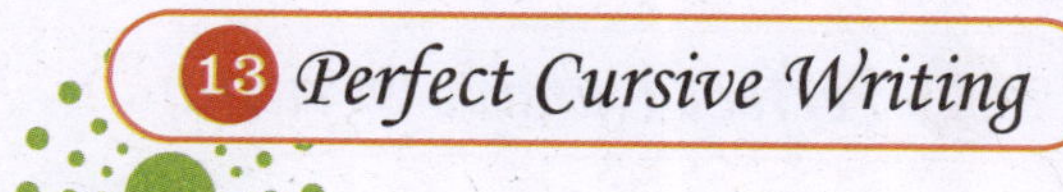

Slow and steady wins the race.

Slow and steady wins the race.

Face is the mirror of mind.

Face is the mirror of mind.

Good mind, good find.

Good mind, good find.

Temperature is the best physic.

Temperature is the best physic.

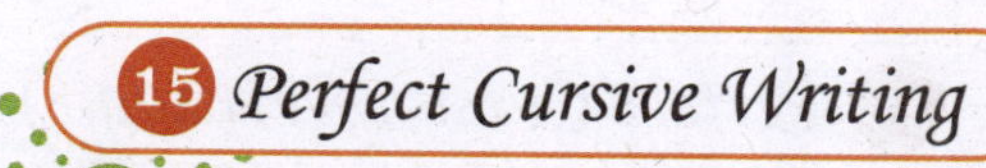

Anger is short madness.

Anger is short madness.

Lying is the matter of violence.

Lying is the matter of violence.

Public voice is God's voice.

Public voice is God's voice.

Beauty need no ornaments.

Beauty need no ornaments.

Early to bed, early to rise.

Early to bed, early to rise.

Charms stike the sight.

Charms stike the sight.

But merit wins to soul.

But merit wins to soul.

Service is no inheritance.

Service is no inheritance.

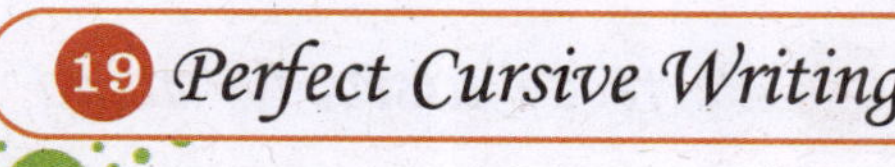

Welcome is the best cheer.

Welcome is the best cheer.

A fair face need no paint.

A fair face need no paint.

Good deeds need no show.

Good mind, good find.

Bear and forbear is good.

Bear and forbear is good.

Fear that man who fears not God.

Fear that man who fears not God.

Never give up hope in despair.

Never give up hope in despair.

Desire of greatness is a goodlike skin.

Desire of greatness is a goodlike skin.

Everything comes to those who can wait.

Everything comes to those who can wait.

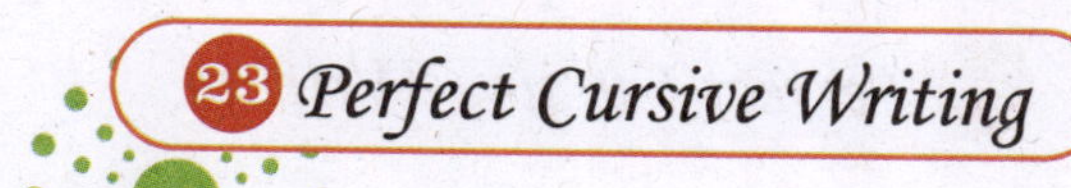

If slavery is not wrong,

If slavery is not wrong,

nothing is wrong.

nothing is wrong.

Noble souls are born to die for others.

Noble souls are born to die for others.

Honest labour bears a lovely face.

Honest labour bears a lovely face.

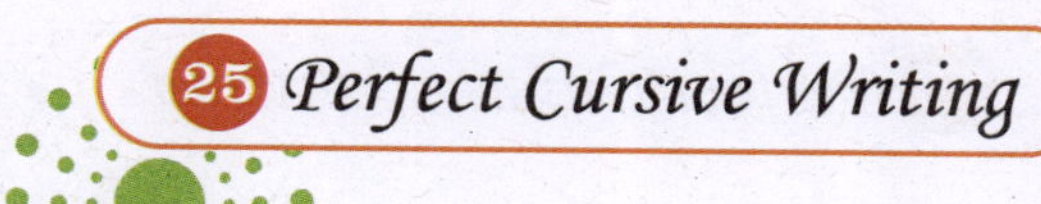

Do your best and leave

Do your best and leave

the rest to God.

the rest to God.

Milk is the food for the Gods.

Milk is the food for the Gods.

Every man has his price.

Every man has his price.

Dealy of justice is injustice.

Dealy of justice is injustice.

Adversity introduces a man to himself.

Adversity introduces a man to himself.

Preserverance is never unfruitful.

Preserverance is never unfruitful.

A good name is better than riches.

A good name is better than riches.

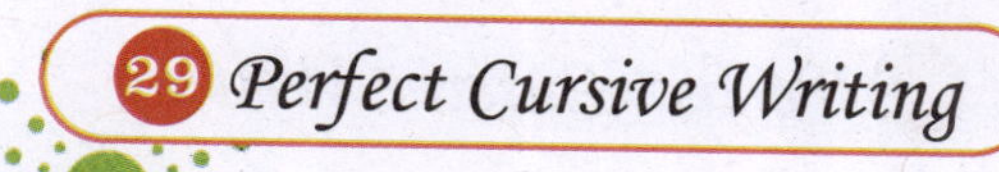

Try and try until you succeed.

Try and try until you succeed.

An empty vessel makes nosie.

An empty vessel makes nosie.

The busy have no time for tears.

The busy have no time for tears.

Rest is the best preparation of work.

Rest is the best preparation of work.

Life is not life at all without delight.

Life is not life at all without delight.

United we stand, divided we fall.

United we stand, divided we fall.

Wisdom is the daughter of all age.

Wisdom is the daughter of all age.

A liar should have a great memory.

A liar should have a great memory.

A stitch in time saves nine.

A stitch in time saves nine.

Killing two birds with one stone.

Killing two birds with one stone.

Better be alone than in a bad company.

Better be alone than in a bad company.

There is no darkness but ignorance.

There is no darkness but ignorance.

A good tongue is a good weapon.

A good tongue is a good weapon.

One flower makes no garland.

One flower makes no garland.

Greaf is the canker of heart.

Greaf is the canker of heart.

When character is lost all is lost.

When character is lost all is lost.

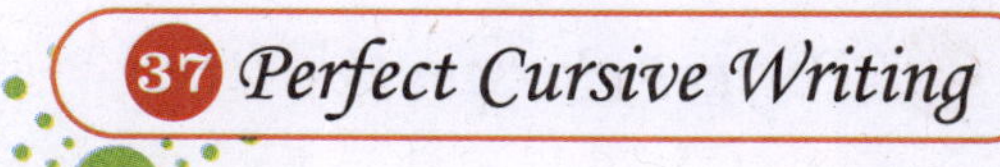

A little pot is soon hot.

A little pot is soon hot.

Do evil and look for like.

Do evil and look for like.

High winds blow on high hills.

High winds blow on high hills.

Inspiration is the greatest prize.

Inspiration is the greatest prize.

Variety created vigour in life.

Variety created vigour in life.

Leisure has its own pleasure.

Leisure has its own pleasure.